GAMES WITH PENCIL AND PAPER

Eric Solomon

Dover Publications, Inc.
New York

Copyright

Published in Canada by General Publishing Company, Ltd., 30 Lesmill Road, Don Mills, Toronto, Ontario.

Bibliographical Note

This Dover edition, first published in 1993, is an unabridged republication of the work first published by Thomas Nelson and Sons Ltd, London, in 1973. A new Preface has been written by the author specially for this edition.

Library of Congress Cataloging-in-Publication Data

Solomon, Eric, 1935–
    Games with pencil and paper / Eric Solomon.
       p.   cm.
    ISBN 0-486-27872-7
    1. Pencil games. I. Title.
    GV1493.S66   1993
    793.73—dc20   93-21327
                                       CIP

Manufactured in the United States of America
Dover Publications, Inc., 31 East 2nd Street, Mineola, N.Y. 11501

Contents

Preface to the Dover Edition

Since *Games with Pencil and Paper* was first published there has been steadily growing interest in board and table games of all sorts. Ernő Rubik's Magic Cube probably attracted more scientific and mathematical attention than any earlier intellectual recreation, and many of those whose enthusiasm was kindled by this puzzle continue to apply their minds to the many unsolved problems of games theory. Of course, *Games with Pencil and Paper* is not intended to contribute to the advancement of scientific knowledge—it aims merely to present the rules for pencil and paper games in a simple and direct way. However, several recent discoveries will be of interest to all players and these are briefly described here. In addition, the omission of several credits is rectified.

Sprouts: This game was introduced by John Horton Conway and M. S. Paterson of Cambridge University. Conway is co-author (with Elwyn R. Berlekamp and Richard K. Guy) of the definitive work on recreational games theory *Winning Ways* (Academic Press, 1982). This lively book contains a section devoted to Sprouts and similar topological games and provides outline proofs confirming my conjecture about the length of the game.

Three-Dimensional Noughts and Crosses: Oren Patashnik has proved (*Mathematics Magazine*, September 1980) that the first player can, in theory, always win this game. His proof required some 750 hours of PDP-10 computer time, but does not affect the enjoyment-value of the game because it is unlikely that any human could be guaranteed to play optimally without very extensive reference tables, in which case he would be unlikely to find an opponent willing to play!

Eleusis: This game is based on the card game invented by Robert Abbott and introduced in Martin Gardner's "Mathematical Games" column in *Scientific American* (June 1959).

Robert has since extended Eleusis in interesting ways, as reported in *Scientific American* (October 1977).

Think of a Letter: This is an old game of unknown origin. In England some players know it as Wordsworth, which is a snappier title for what I consider to be the best of all word games. The game is improved if five-letter words carry a bonus of five points rather than one point as described in this book.

Crystals: I have received many enquiries about the origin of Crystals and must now admit to having devised the game specially for this book.

Hex: Hex is the invention of the Danish poet and polymath Piet Hein, who also invented the Soma Cube puzzle. The game was first shown in 1942 under the name Polygon and about ten years later was marketed by Parker under the name Hex.

Middleman: This is an adaptation of a variety of trading games based on the behavior of free markets.

Boxes: No one seems to know how this game originated. It is well described and analysed in *Winning Ways* (see *Sprouts,* above).

Coincidences: This game is based on a vague memory of a similar game that I played as a child—and for which I can find no references. Players of the later code-breaking game Mastermind (Vic-Toy, 1972) may notice some similarities.

Aggression: Aggression was inspired by the unabashedly bellicose board game of world conquest marketed under the name of Risk (Parker, 1953), though the mechanics are quite different.

Battleships: Hubert Phillips, the inventor of the version presented here, was a popular broadcaster, puzzle compiler, and writer on games in the 1940s.

Subterfuge: This is a pencil and paper adaptation of my board game War Office Papers marketed as Sigma File (Seven Towns, 1970) and subsequently under different names by various manufacturers.

Other Games: Games not listed above are traditional games of unknown origin.

Eric Solomon

Introduction

The games described here require no more equipment than pencils and paper. Some are old favourites, some are well-established games which deserve to be better known and some are brand-new games. Each chapter describes one game in a roughly uniform fashion. A short background to the game is followed by a specification of the rules. Next comes an illustrative game if appropriate and feasible within the limitations of space. Finally, the strategy of the game is briefly discussed.

Any method of deciding which player makes the first move will suffice provided it gives everyone an equal chance: if there are two players a coin may be tossed; if there are more than two people involved write the numbers 1, 2, 3, etc. on separate pieces of paper and draw them out of a hat or cup. The player drawing 1 will move first, 2 moves second, and so on.

The facts that word-game players increase their vocabularies, that positional-game players improve their visuo-spatial predictive capabilities, or whatever psychology buzz-words are currently in fashion for pattern-spotting ability, are beneficial side effects of what should be enjoyable pastimes. Not all games bestow these blessings on their participants, however, and there's no telling what traits a game such as Subterfuge will develop! So do remember that games should be played for fun.

I should like to acknowledge the assistance afforded by Neil Peppé, and other friends, including the long-suffering games section of the London Inter Varsity Club, on whom many experimental games have been inflicted.

E.S.

Sprouts

A "topological" game

Topology is the branch of mathematics which deals with relationships between parts of an object not affected by the size or distortions of the object. Sprouts was devised quite recently at Cambridge University specifically as a purely "topological" game. The name derives from the appearance of the completed game, which resembles nothing so much as the plan of an over-cooked and disintegrating sprout. The game is suitable for two or three players but is not recommended for more unless a rubber is played in which every player is given a first move.

Before play starts some points are drawn at random on a sheet of paper. Five or six points make for a game lasting about five minutes. More points give a longer game. The players take turns to draw a smooth line starting and ending on a point, then draw one new point somewhere on the line. There are two rules:

1 No line may cross any other line.
2 No point may have more than three lines leaving it.

Note that the new points added after the game is under way always begin life with two lines leaving them. That is, the new line drawn by a player is effectively divided into two lines when he adds his point. From Rule 2 we can see that only one new line may be started or ended at one of the points drawn after the game has begun. Also note that it's perfectly permissible for a line to start and end on the same point provided the rules above are satisfied.

The winner is the player who takes the final move and leaves no opportunity for another player to complete a valid turn.

The three figures show positions in the middle of a 5-point game. Fig. 1 illustrates two valid moves with the new lines dotted and the starting points shaded. The figures 2 and 3 show invalid moves, also dotted.

When you have played several short games and become familiar with the rules you can try a larger number of starting points, say ten. Although the original points are placed randomly it's advisable to space them out well to avoid congestion towards the end of a game.

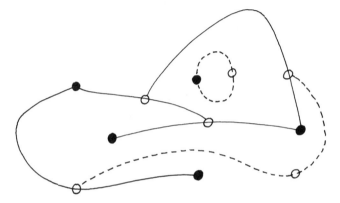

Figure 1   Two Valid Moves in a 5-point Game of Sprouts

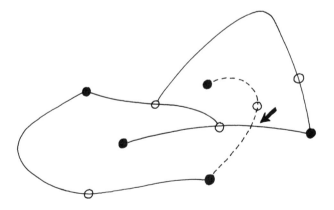

Figure 2   An Invalid Move   —   Lines cross

Strategy: Very little is known about winning strategy in Sprouts. If you have aspirations to crack this problem the following facts might be useful:

a Every new line (pair of lines really as the new point divides it in two) either produces one new *region*, or it joins two hitherto separate *parts* of the game. The term "region" is used for a closed area of the paper bounded by lines.

b There is a relationship linking the number of points, lines, regions and separate parts of a game. This equation is true at all times during a game:
POINTS + REGIONS = LINES + PARTS
This is known as Euler's formula and was discovered about two hundred years before Sprouts was invented!

c It is conjectured that a game of Sprouts always has a number of moves equal to or greater than twice the number of starting points, and less than three times the number of starting points.

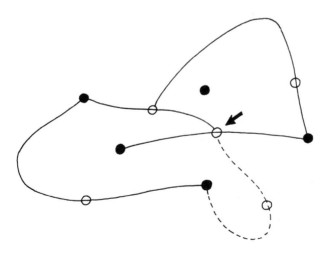

Figure 3 An Invalid Move – Too many lines on a point

Three-Dimensional
Noughts and Crosses

A spatial pattern game

Noughts and crosses, or Tic-Tac-Toe, is a game of limited scope. For instance, it has the property that the second player can always force a draw however the first player moves. As such, it is at best a test of endurance. The ordinary game is played on a single three by three framework of squares in two dimensions. A logical step in finding an improved game was to try playing it in three dimensions on a board with depth as well as height and width. The "3D" game described here has been popular at universities and among computer programmers for over ten years. It is a first-class game and deserves to be better known. In recent years some "hardware" versions have appeared on the market, but the game can be played perfectly adequately on paper. Indeed this is how it was originally played.

Imagine a cube made up of 64 smaller cubes stacked so that there are four layers of sixteen cubes. Each layer has four rows of four cubes as shown in Fig. 1. In order to play the game on paper the layers are separated and drawn as illustrated.

The two players alternately write their symbols into the boxes in the usual way with the "cross" player starting. The first person to obtain four of his symbols in a straight line is the winner. A straight line, that is, in the properly stacked cube. Fig. 2 shows some completed games with the winning lines shaded. Note that the boundary line round each layer is not normally drawn.

Strategy : There's a rich field for investigation here. The important squares are those which have most lines passing

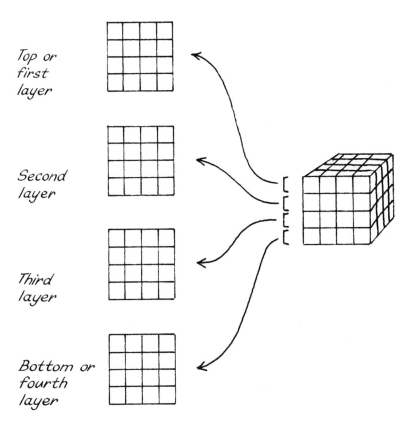

Top or
first
layer

Second
layer

Third
layer

Bottom or
fourth
layer

Figure 1   *Derivation of the Game Sheet for*
3D Noughts and Crosses

through them. It's obviously good tactics to occupy some of these squares early in the game. Fig. 3 shows a game sheet with the number of lines passing through each square indicated in the square itself.

A useful exercise for the serious student of this game is to take one layer of the cube and to try to establish what majority of symbols will guarantee him a win inside the layer chosen.

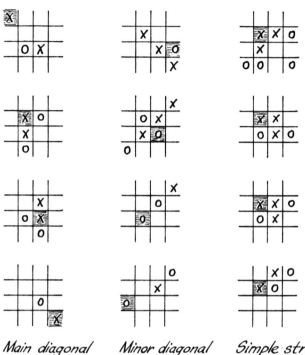

Main diagonal across the cube. *Minor diagonal across a layer.* *Simple straight vertically through the cube.*

(There is a deliberate mistake in one of these games. The losing player has not noticed that he has a completed line. Can you find it?)

Figure 2   Some Completed Games of 3D Noughts and Crosses

7	4	4	7
4	4	4	4
4	4	4	4
7	4	4	7

4	4	4	4
4	7	7	4
4	7	7	4
4	4	4	4

4	4	4	4
4	7	7	4
4	7	7	4
4	4	4	4

7	4	4	7
4	4	4	4
4	4	4	4
7	4	4	7

Figure 3 Relative Importance of Squares in
3D Noughts and Crosses

Eleusis

An "induction" game

Eleusis started life as a card game of a novel sort. Practically all games are deductive in that the players learn a set of rules and deduce their best moves within these rules. In Eleusis one player secretly invents a rule and the others make trial moves in order to discover what the rule is. That is, they try to *induce* the general rule from their particular moves. The inventor of the rule, called the "Umpire", tells each player whether his trial move is successful or not, but he may impart no further information. One attraction of the game is its analogy with the process of scientific research: the scientist observes particular facts then postulates general laws of nature which could explain the facts. The player of Eleusis observes the success or failure of his trial moves, and those of the other players, and postulates a law to explain them.

There are several inductive games based on Eleusis. The version described here can be played by two, three or four players. A game consists of a number of rounds, as many as there are players. In each round one player takes the part of the Umpire. At the end of a round the players, including the Umpire, assess their penalty points. When every player has been Umpire once the game finishes and the person with the lowest total of penalty points is the winner.

Equipment: Each player requires a sheet of paper having a 10-by-10 matrix of squares as shown in Fig. 1. A player's paper is used for the round in which he is Umpire. The player on the Umpire's left is the "A" player, the player opposite is the "B" player and the player to his right the "C" player. If there are only three players the "C" position is not used. Similarly, if there are only two players one is the Umpire and the other the "A" player. The "lettered" players each have appropriate letters as shown in Fig. 1. The

Umpire has twenty symbols and numbers as shown and at the start of each cycle of play, immediately before the "A" player takes his turn, he must circle the next symbol or number starting on the left of the top row and finishing at the right of the bottom row.

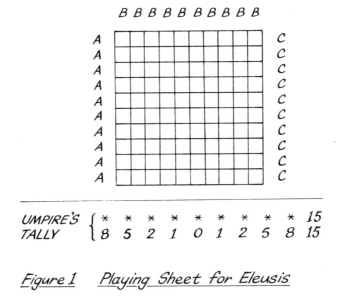

Figure 1   Playing Sheet for Eleusis

A Move : The "A" player takes a turn by placing the point of his pencil on a square of his choosing and asking if he may place a letter A in it. The square must be empty at this stage. If the Umpire replies "Yes" the player writes a letter A in the square and crosses out one of the A letters on his side of the sheet. If the Umpire replies "No" the turn passes to the "B" player, and the "A" player is not entitled to cross out one of his letters. The "B" and "C" players play in the same way by asking if they may place, respectively, a B or C in some square.

Penalty points : A round ends immediately one of the players "goes out" by using his last letter. If no player has gone out by the end of cycle 20 the round is terminated. This is easily detected as the Umpire will find that he has no more numbers to circle. At the end of the round the letter players count their unused letters which are reckoned as penalty points. A player who has gone out will have no penalty points for that round. The Umpire's penalty is the number he last circled.

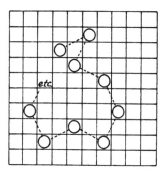

C	A	B	C	A	B
B	A	B	C	A	C
A	C	A→B	B	A
C	B←A←C	C	B
B	A	C	B	A	C

First letter anywhere – next letter must be a chess-knight's move from previous letter.

Spiral of the letters ABCABC, etc. The letters can be placed in any order so long as their position is correct.

Figure 2   Typical Umpire's Rules in Eleusis

It will be seen from Fig. 1 that the Umpire receives no penalty points if the round lasts exactly fifteen cycles. He is heavily penalised if he thinks of a rule so easy to discover that someone goes out at cycle 10, or soon after. Similarly he is penalised for thinking out a rule which no one can discover before the full twenty cycles are played.

The Umpire's rule : There's absolutely no restriction on this. To minimise his penalty points the Umpire should devise a rule which at least one player will discover after five trial move failures. Typically the letter players will have a certain amount of luck before they find the rule, so it's unlikely that these failures will all occur in the first five cycles.

The Umpire should write his rule down in some way, if only to avoid disputes. The best way is probably to complete a spare sheet with the letters placed in the appropriate squares. Obviously he should avoid "silly" rules such as "A may be placed anywhere, B and C on the edge only"! It is important that a rule should not favour one letter player more than any other. Some versions of Eleusis try to avoid this possibility by augmenting the Umpire's penalty points by the difference between the round-winners' penalty points and those of the runner-up. Fig. 2 shows some specimen rules which may inspire further ideas.

Think of a Letter

A "crossword" game

This is one of the very best word games and has been popular in England for many years. Some people call it Crosswords.

It can be played by from two to five people. Each player is issued with a pencil and a sheet of paper having a five-by-five framework of squares. After it has been decided who starts, the first player calls out one letter which he writes into some chosen square of his framework. Each of the other players writes the *same letter* into some square on his own paper. The second player then calls out a letter of his choice which everyone again places in his framework. When all the players have taken a turn in this way the first player calls out another letter, and so it goes until all 25 squares have been filled. The object of the game is to spell out words reading either across or down the sheet. No player should permit any other player to see his framework until the game is finished.

Each player accumulates a score as follows:

1 For every word, either across or down, as many points are scored as there are letters in the word. One-letter words, however, score nothing.
2 Five-letter words score a bonus point.

No two words in the same row, or column, may share letters. For example, suppose a row contained the letters I T W I T. The IT scores two points, the word WIT scores three points, and the total for the row is five points. It would not be permitted to score the two points for IT as well as the four points for the word TWIT. It is important that all players should record a letter clearly in its square before the next letter is called.

Every player adds his row totals and his column totals

together to obtain his final score. The player with the highest final score is the winner.

Fig. 1 shows two completed sheets from the same game with the row, column and total scores recorded along the right-hand edge, the lower edge, and the bottom right-hand corner respectively for each sheet.

C	S	S	J	O	2
V	E	N	A	L	6
T	X	A	W	E	3
H	E	R	R	S	4
A	D	E	P	T	6
2	6	6	3	4	(42)

N	O	S	H	S	4
T	A	P	E	D	6
S	R	E	R	L	2
J	A	W	E	V	3
E	X	A	C	T	6
0	3	4	4	0	(32)

Figure 1   Two Completed Sheets from a Game of Think of a Letter

Permissible words: As in the majority of word games there is the possibility of dispute over the matter of which words are permissible. These are easily resolved if the players agree beforehand to use a particular dictionary. As a rule, proper nouns requiring a capital letter, hyphenated words and words including an apostrophe, such as DON'T, should be avoided. Needless to say, reference to the dictionary before the playing sheets are completed is strictly forbidden.

Variations: Think of a Letter is capable of much variation: the reader should feel free to try a larger playing area, say 8 by 8 squares, if he wants a longer game. You may decide to reward longer words more generously. For example, an eight-letter word could merit two bonus points.

Crystals

A pattern-visualising game

Here is a game played on squared paper in which each contestant tries to "grow" crystals. The winner is the person who covers most squares with his crystals. The game can be played by any number of people, but the greater the number of players the harder it is to form crystals, and those that are produced tend to be less spectacular. The playing area may be any size and shape but a piece of paper having 21 rows of 21 squares each is recommended as a standard.

Symmetry: All perfect crystals display symmetry in some form or other. Many are manifestly three-dimensional. Under certain conditions, however, some substances form plate-like two-dimensional crystals, the sort we shall be growing in this game. Before proceeding it is important to understand the concept of a "mirror axis of symmetry". This sounds frighteningly esoteric but it's simply an imaginary line drawn across the crystal and along which it could be folded so that the two halves exactly overlay each other. A tidy housewife would fold a tablecloth along its mirror axis.

The symmetry of our crystals is dictated to a degree by the nature of squared paper. The "natural" axes to use are those parallel to the lines on the paper. If we used only these two axes it would be simple to construct crystals according to the rules of the game. Too simple, in fact, to offer any challenge. The best axes are the two natural axes plus the two diagonal axes. Thus, it must be possible to fold each crystal horizontally, vertically and diagonally across its centre-point without obtaining any protruding or uncovered sections. The H-shaped crystal shown in Fig. 2 would be permissible if only the natural axes were used, but it does not have sufficient symmetry when the diagonal axes are introduced. The crystals shown in Fig. 1 have symmetry about all four axes.

Atoms : Crystals are grown from atoms. Each player has one type of atom and at the start of play decides on a suitable symbol to represent it. With two players one could use noughts and the other crosses, while a third player might use small triangles. Having decided who is to have first move the players take turns to draw one of their atoms in any square not already occupied. This is called "seeding". A crystal may be grown as soon as it contains four seed-atoms. You might be excused for asking "Which crystal? Where?" The answer is any crystal you can visualise on the paper, and which satisfies the crystal-growing rules below. The crystal is "marked" by drawing a heavy pencil line around the boundary and roughly shading the interior. The number of squares within the crystal is counted and added to its owner's score. The game then continues with the next player placing a seed-atom.

Crystal rules : To be legitimate a crystal must satisfy the following rules:

1 The crystal must contain four or more atoms of one type and none of any other type.
2 The crystal must be symmetric with respect to the vertical, horizontal and two diagonal axes passing through its centre point.
3 The crystal must be properly connected. Atoms cannot be connected by their corners only.
4 The crystal must contain no empty holes.
5 The crystal must have no "interlock" boundaries.

The last condition merely means that crystals must never lock like jigsaw pieces. Figs 1 and 2 show permissible and impermissible crystals. Study of these will soon clarify the notion of interlock boundaries.

The game ends when everyone agrees that no more crystals can be grown. The player with the largest score is the winner. If the crystal shading is done distinctively the scores may readily be checked at the end of the game.

To develop your skill rapidly the points in the next section should be noted. Fig. 3 exhibits a specimen game between two players who have kindly numbered their seed-atoms to show the order in which they were placed.

Points of strategy : The formation of a crystal leaves you less strongly represented by seed-atoms than your opponents. This effect becomes proportionally less noticeable as the number of un-crystallised seed-atoms increases. Therefore it may not necessarily be advantageous to make crystals as soon as they are possible.

The non-starting player or players should place their atoms defensively at first because the starter's potential for really large paper-filling crystals is high after four or five rounds of play. If there are only two players it's highly probable that the starter will form the first crystal. In this case the non-starter should concentrate on restricting the size of his opponent's first crystal.

Long spiky crystals do not score heavily but are effective in preventing the opponent from forming large crystals.

In any legally formed crystal every atom has a special property which it may be useful to note: suppose the atoms of a crystal, whether seed-atoms or ones "implied" after the crystal boundary has been drawn, could migrate from one square to any other within the crystal. It must be possible for any atom to "walk" in a straight line to one of the symmetry axes without leaving the crystal at any point or touching a boundary. Having reached the axis the wandering atom must be able to turn through an angle of *not more than* 45 degrees to face the centre of the crystal along the axis it has reached. If it decided to walk to the centre along this axis it could do so without leaving the crystal on its way and without touching a boundary.

The facing illustrations and that on the following page give examples of permissible and impermissible crystals.

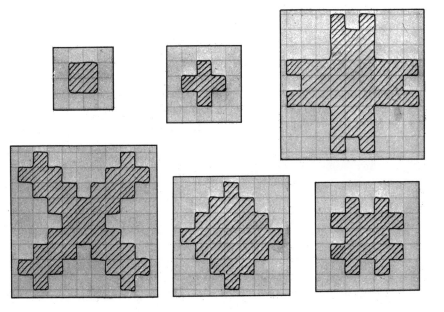

Figure 1   *Some Permissible Crystals*

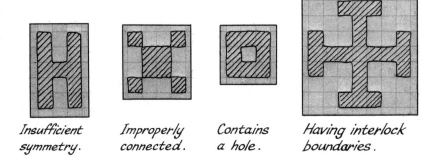

| *Insufficient symmetry.* | *Improperly connected.* | *Contains a hole.* | *Having interlock boundaries.* |

Figure 2   *Some Impermissible Crystals*

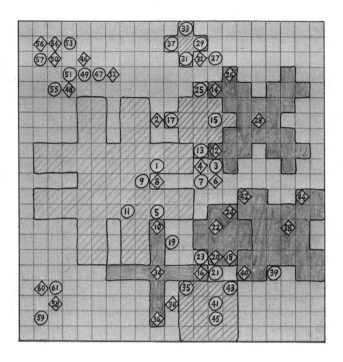

SCORE

O	◇
73	12
13	29
5	13
16	28
107	82

Player ◇
conceded the game
after
move 61

Figure 3   _A game of Crystals with the atoms
numbered to show the order of play_

Hex

A curious race game

Hex is a race game for two players. It is played on a tri-angular grid, as illustrated. Paper marked in this way is obtainable from good stationers and is sometimes known as "isometric graph paper". To play Hex, the participants take turns to mark one previously unmarked point of their choice. These points are located at the intersections of the lines. One player marks his points with a circle, the other with a heavy dot, the object of the game being to connect two opposite sides of the playing area with a line of adjacent symbols. Two symbols are adjacent if there is just one short line connecting them. The first player to construct a complete line with his symbols wins the game. Note, however, that his line must connect the correct pair of opposing sides. One player aims to connect one pair of sides and the other tries to connect the other pair of sides. Which pair of sides is allocated to which

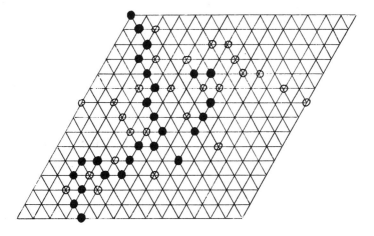

Figure 1 _Hex Sheet showing a Win for the "Dot" Player_

player is decided at the start of the game. Each corner point is regarded as belonging to both of the sides meeting it. Two lines of marked points cannot cross because this would imply that at least one point was marked with both symbols. It follows that there cannot be a draw in Hex.

The playing area : The sheet may be of any size, a larger playing area makes for a longer game. It is vital to ensure that each side of the sheet has the same number of points.

If you are unable to obtain pre-printed isometric graph paper a sheet may be constructed quite easily from ordinary lined writing paper. It is possible to do this free-hand but a ruler should be used for one set of parallel lines at least. These should be drawn at sixty degrees to the printed lines on the sheet. The angle can be measured with a protractor or by using a pair of compasses to construct a large equilateral triangle with its base along one of the printed lines. It's quite feasible to guess the sixty-degree angle with some practice. Small inaccuracies in registering the lines are not important.

A sheet can be used several times if drawn in ink and if play is conducted with pencils applied without undue pressure. The marks can then be erased at the end of each game.

Strategy : It's best to start the game with fairly well separated marks and gradually to fill in the intervening spaces as the game progresses. It is known that the opening player can, in theory, always win the game. This fact, while reassuring, doesn't indicate how he is to do it in practice. Certain "constellations" of symbols can always be safely connected however the opponent plays. A simple example is afforded by a pair of symbols at either end of a lozenge made up of two small triangles. Provided the remaining points of the lozenge are free from enemy symbols they can always be connected. Any aspiring "Hex maniac" would be well advised to discover these safe constellations by experimentation.

Middleman

A trading game

Business games are becoming very popular. There are now national competitions and many corporations use them in the training of young executives. Middleman bears little resemblance to the complex games used for these purposes, but it does incorporate such basic decisions as how much to buy, how much to sell and at what prices.

Starting: The players, of which there may be any number, take the part of traders dealing in tins of some worthy commodity, say sardines. Each starts with a fixed sum of money and then buys and sells tins of the product with the object of ending the game with more money than his competitors. The supply and demand of tins must obviously be limited, and limited in a variable way. Since dice are not acceptable in true pencil-and-paper games the market figures are decided by adding together numbers privately chosen by the players at the start of the game. Let's call these A and D numbers. A stands for "available tins" and D for "demand for tins". On his game sheet, see Fig. 7, each player writes the numbers 0 to 9 into the boxes on the row marked A, but he may write them *in any order he chooses*. Next he writes the same numbers in a different order into the boxes on the row marked D.

The amount of money allocated to each player is ten times the number of persons involved. The units are pounds, dollars or any other unit of currency but are not quoted here as they are irrelevant to the playing of the game. Thus, if there are two players each starts with twenty units, if there are three each starts with thirty, and so on. This figure is written into the first CASH box in the first column of the game sheet. Zero is written into the TINS box beneath and then you're ready to start.

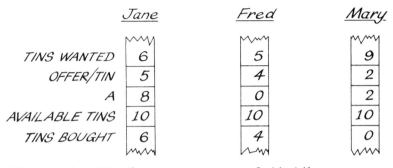

	Jane	Fred	Mary
TINS WANTED	6	5	9
OFFER/TIN	5	4	2
A	8	0	2
AVAILABLE TINS	10	10	10
TINS BOUGHT	6	4	0

Figure 1   The Auction stage of Middleman – First Example

Game-turns : All the players first visit an auction to buy tins. Each privately writes the number of tins he wants to buy into the TINS WANTED box of the current column on his sheet. (All players start in the first column, and when this is complete move to the second column, and so on.) Next he writes the amount of money he is prepared to pay per tin into the OFFER/TIN box. These two numbers constitute the player's order. After each player has written his order the auctioneer— not one of the players but purely conceptual— reveals how many tins are for sale, which is obtained by each player calling out his A number. These are added together to give the total number available. Now our notional auctioneer is like anyone else in that he wants to maximise his profit. He therefore favours the player who has offered the most money per tin, and the player has his order fulfilled as far as possible. If his order is completely satisfied and there are tins still available the player with the next highest offer per tin has his order dealt with. The procedure goes like this until either all orders are met or there are no tins left to be sold. Each player next writes the number of tins he has succeeded in buying in the next box marked TINS BOUGHT. Here is an example of the auction stage of the game: we have three players— Jane, Fred and Mary. The relevant parts of their game sheets are shown in Fig. 1. Jane has offered most per tin, Fred is next and Mary has tried to get her tins too cheap with the result that she gets none at all.

When two or more players have made identical offers per tin, and no other player with a higher offer is still waiting for his order to be met, the tie is resolved by satisfying their orders equally until one of the following situations occurs.

a One or more of the players has his order completely satisfied, in which case the auction continues in the normal way. That is, tins are sold to the player with the highest offer price who still has an unfulfilled order. Again, if there is more than one player due to buy tins, and if several players have identical "best" offers, they share tins equally until one of the situations listed occurs.

b More than one of the "best-offer" players still want tins but the remaining tins cannot be shared equally between them. That's to say there are fewer tins than "best-offer" players so that they can't receive even one tin each. In this case these players drop out of the auction and the tins remaining are then offered to the next highest bidder.

c There are no tins left to be sold, at which point the auction stage is ended.

Here are two more examples showing what happens when there are players offering the same amount for tins:

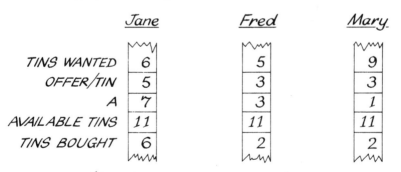

	Jane	Fred	Mary
TINS WANTED	6	5	9
OFFER/TIN	5	3	3
A	7	3	1
AVAILABLE TINS	11	11	11
TINS BOUGHT	6	2	2

(One tin remains unsold because it cannot be shared equally by Fred and Mary and there is no other buyer remaining.)

Figure 2   The Auction Stage of Middleman –
Second Example

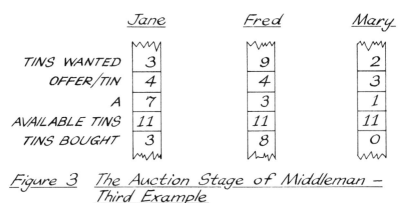

	Jane	Fred	Mary
TINS WANTED	3	9	2
OFFER/TIN	4	4	3
A	7	3	1
AVAILABLE TINS	11	11	11
TINS BOUGHT	3	8	0

Figure 3   The Auction Stage of Middleman –
Third Example

When all the players have filled in their TINS BOUGHT boxes they proceed to fill the CASH and TINS boxes at the head of the selling stage of the game sheets. In the CASH box a player will write a sum equal to the cash in hand minus the money he has just spent in acquiring new tins. The latter amount is, of course, the product of the number of tins bought and the offer price per tin. If he finds that he does not have enough money to pay for his new tins he is bankrupt and eliminated from the game. This situation can occur only through error in placing an order. In the TINS box each player writes a number equal to the sum of his original tins and the number of new tins. All is now ready for the selling stage.

Selling : Everyone privately decides how many tins to put on the market and the asking price per tin. These numbers are written in the FOR SALE and the PRICE/TIN boxes. Notice that the market will never pay more than 10 per tin. If any player has asked for 11 or more per tin it counts as if he had written 10 in the PRICE/TIN box. The D numbers are then added together to give the number of tins that the market demands. This is written in every player's DEMAND box.

How do we discover how many tins each player manages to sell? The method is identical to that used in the auction stage, except that whereas the Auctioneer favoured players *offering the "highest" price per tin*, the market favours those *asking the "lowest" price per tin*. The player asking the lowest price sells all his marketed tins unless the market wants less.

If two or more players have asked identical prices for their tins, and there is no other player with a lower asking price who still has unsold tins, the tie is resolved by allowing them to sell tins equally until one of the following situations occurs:

a One or more of the players has sold all his tins, in which case the sale continues in the normal way, tins being sold by the player with the lowest asking price who still has tins on the market. Again, if there are several players with the same asking price they sell tins equally until one of the situations listed here occurs.

b More than one of the "cheapest price" players still have tins to sell but the market wants less tins, so they cannot sell an equal number of tins each. In this case these players withdraw their unsold tins from the market and the next cheapest tins are sold.

c The market requires no more tins, in which case the sale is closed.

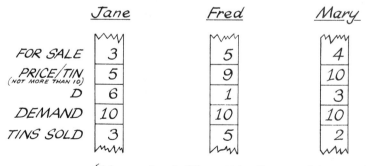

	Jane	Fred	Mary
FOR SALE	3	5	4
PRICE/TIN (NOT MORE THAN 10)	5	9	10
D	6	1	3
DEMAND	10	10	10
TINS SOLD	3	5	2

(Mary is left with 2 unsold tins.)

Figure 4 The Selling Stage of Middleman – First Example

Three examples of the selling stage of the game are given in Figures 4, 5 and 6. The last two examples illustrate cases where different players have specified the same asking price.

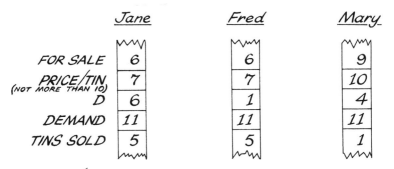

	Jane	Fred	Mary
FOR SALE	6	6	9
PRICE/TIN (NOT MORE THAN 10)	7	7	10
D	6	1	4
DEMAND	11	11	11
TINS SOLD	5	5	1

(The remaining tin demanded by the market after Jane and Fred have sold 5 tins each cannot be provided equally by both Jane and Fred, so Mary is allowed to provide it.)

Figure 5 The Selling Stage of Middleman - Second Example

	Jane	Fred	Mary
FOR SALE	3	4	22
PRICE/TIN (NOT MORE THAN 10)	5	9	9
D	6	1	4
DEMAND	11	11	11
TINS SOLD	3	4	4

(The market demand has been satisfied and Mary is left with 18 unsold tins.)

Figure 6 The Selling Stage of Middleman — Third Example

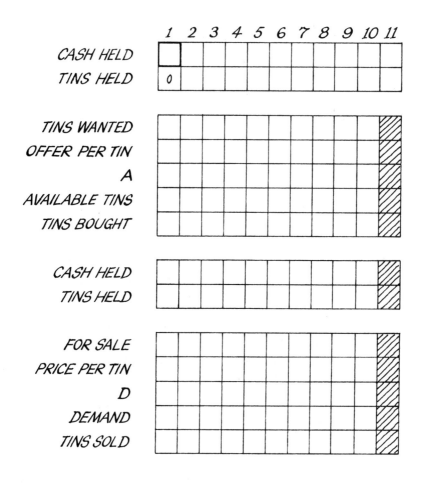

Figure 7   The Game Sheet for Middleman

When everyone has recorded the number of tins sold in the TINS SOLD box the round is finished and the CASH and TINS boxes at the head of the next column can be filled in. In the CASH box goes the amount in the previous CASH box plus the revenue from sales. The latter quantity is the product of the number of tins sold and the asking price per tin. The TINS box contains the number of tins held at the start of the selling stage minus the number of tins actually sold.

Winning : The winner is the person with the most money in the CASH box at the head of column 11. That is, the final column of the game sheet which is not completed beyond the CASH and TINS boxes. The number of tins still held does *not* enter the reckoning. The final selling stage of the game is obviously important as everyone will be trying hard to sell their remaining tins.

Game-sheet : Fig. 7 presents a full game sheet which can be prepared easily on ordinary lined writing paper. A de-luxe version can be produced by writing or typing the text in the left-hand margin on a narrow strip of cardboard clipped into place on a sheet of lined paper.

Strategy : The art of playing Middleman well is to recognise which rounds provide buyer's markets and which provide seller's markets, and to buy and sell accordingly. One of the interesting features is that a certain amount of prediction is possible on the basis of your A and D numbers and the, so far revealed, A and D numbers of your opponents. It's rare to get a good buyer's and a good seller's market in the same round so it's often necessary to buy a lot of tins in one round and to hold on to them until a seller's market comes up. However, it is easy to delay too long, with the result that when an even better buyer's market occurs you have no spare cash with which to bid for tins.

Boxes

An "enclosing" game

This game for two players has always been very popular. It's commonly found, however, that Rule 2, below, is ignored, which is a pity because it greatly enhances the game.

The players use one sheet of plain paper previously marked with a rectangular framework of dots, as shown in Fig. 1. The dots are destined to be connected together to form a grid, such as that shown in Fig. 2. The size of the playing area is immaterial though it's preferable to have an odd number of squares, or "boxes", in the completed grid. To obtain this result there should be an even number of dots along each side of the initial playing area. The object of the game is to win the greater number of boxes.

A game turn : The players take turns to draw one horizontal or vertical line connecting two adjacent and previously unconnected dots. A box is won by that player who draws the fourth and last side of the box. After a player has won a box he writes his initial into the box and immediately takes a further turn. This next turn may also win a box, in which case he would be entitled to take yet another turn. In this way it is possible for a player to win a considerable number of boxes before his opponent may take his turn. The following conditions must be observed :

1 After winning a box a player *must* draw one more line immediately. It's possible for one line to win two boxes at once but the player takes only one further turn.
2 It is *not* compulsory to win a box even though there may be a square with three of its sides completed.

The figures : Fig. 1 shows a game in progress on a 63-box sheet. Fig. 2 shows the same game completed. Player "A" has won 33 boxes and player "B" has won 30, so "A" wins by three.

Strategy : Towards the end of a game there occur configurations of lines called "corridors". These are of two types, "open", and "closed". An open corridor is illustrated at the bottom right-hand corner of Fig. 1. It contains four squares (uncompleted boxes). If a player connects two dots in the corridor it becomes a closed corridor and the other player can, if he wishes, win all the boxes in the corridor on his next turn. A closed corridor is shown at the top left-hand corner of Fig. 1. The strategy of the game involves yielding small closed corridors to your opponent and winning large ones yourself. Rule 2 is important here, for suppose that a game

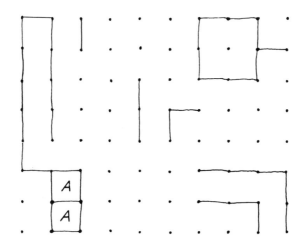

Figure 1   Game Sheet for Boxes with Game in Progress

was finished except for a small closed corridor and a larger open one: if you decided to win the whole of the closed corridor your final line would have to close the larger open corridor and your opponent would then win it all. If, on the other hand, you were to leave two squares of the original closed corridor

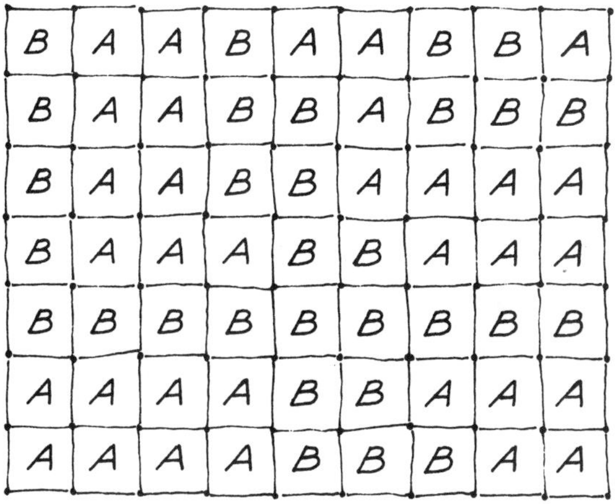

B	A	A	B	A	A	B	B	A
B	A	A	B	B	A	B	B	B
B	A	A	B	B	A	A	A	A
B	A	A	A	B	B	A	A	A
B	B	B	B	B	B	B	B	B
A	A	A	A	B	B	A	A	A
A	A	A	A	B	B	B	A	A

Figure 2   Completed Game of Boxes

uncompleted your opponent would be forced to close the open corridor at the end of his next turn, and you could then win it all for yourself.

Note that corridors do not necessarily have to have two "ends". The square formation at the top right-hand corner of Fig. 1 is an open corridor as the addition of one more line will produce a set of four squares which could be won by the next player.

Coincidences

A word game

A game does not necessarily have to be fair to be enjoyable. Coincidences is one of these "unfair" games and so long as this is recognised by the players from the outset it will provide much fun and lively argument. Any number can play the game, which is divided into a number of rounds. In each round one of the players acts as "Accountant". The first thing the accountant does is to think of a word of about six letters. He secretly records the word on a piece of paper and announces the number of letters it contains. The other players attempt to discover his word by calling out sequences of letters of equal length to the accountant's word. All the accountant has to do is to count up the number of coincident letters in the last sequence called and state the result. He must not say where in his word the coincidences occur. For example, suppose the accountant's word is YELLOW and that the sequence called out by one of the players is EEEOOO. The second and fifth letters coincide so the accountant simply replies "two". The players take turns to call out a sequence with the player on the accountant's left starting the proceedings. When some player calls out a sequence which exactly matches the accountant's word the round ends and a score is recorded as follows.

Scoring : The player spelling out the accountant's word receives two points, the other players receiving one point each. The accountant also scores as follows: if his word is discovered in fewer trial sequences than there are letters in his word he scores nothing. After this he is entitled to a score of one point until the number of sequences called is equal to twice the number of letters, at which point his score rises to two. When the number of sequences equals three times the number of words the accountant scores three and so on.

As an example, suppose the accountant's word was CEN-TURY and that it was found on the fifteenth trial sequence. The player calling CENTURY receives two points, the other players one point each, while the accountant receives two points. When all rounds have been played everyone totals their round-scores and the person with the highest result is the winner.

Word restrictions: As in the majority of word games the accountant should not choose proper nouns normally spelt with a capital letter, technical terms unlikely to be known to the other players or hyphenated words. There is no restriction whatsoever on the sequences called out by the other players.

Recording sequences: Each player should record his own trial sequences, and those of the other players in some sort of table. The sample game below shows tables in which the number of coincidences is written against each sequence. Circled letters are those which the player firmly believes to be in the Accountant's word.

Sample game: In this game there were two participants, A and B. Thus there were two rounds with A acting as accountant in the first round and B as accountant in the second round.

Strategy: It can be seen that there is considerable scope for skill in the game of Coincidences. On one hand there is the mathematical problem of efficiently permuting the letters to obtain matchings as quickly as possible. On the other hand the game calls for the "literary" ability of recognising words from a skeleton of their letters. Notice that in the sample game both players endeavour to find vowels as early as possible. In round 1 player B had a lucky inspiration at trial 9. In round 2 player A had to work hard to discover the first letter once he had deduced that UDDLE were the last five letters.

An elementary knowledge of letter frequency in English words is necessary to play well. It's also useful to know the

Round 1

A's word is
WHISKY

Round 2

B's word is
PUDDLE

E E E E E E
I I I I I I
S I S I S I
I S I S I S
I S T T T T
T T (I)(S) T T
R R I S H R
L L I S L L
(W)(H) I S (K)(Y)

Score in round 1:

Accountant A scores
$\frac{9}{6}$ = 1 point
Player B scores 2

I I I I I I
S E S E S E
E E S E E S
A S E S S E
O O O O O (E)
U U U U U E
A U A U A E
B (U) B R A E
B U B A D E
L U L L L E
T U T L L E
H U N D L E
C U R (D)(L) E
C U (D) D L E
F U D D L E
H U D D L E
M U D D L E
P U D D L E

Score in round 2:

Accountant B scores
$\frac{18}{6}$ = 3 points
Player A scores 2

B wins the game with a total of 5 points.
A has scored a total of 3 points.

Figure 1   Sample Game of Coincidences

most common digrams (pairs of letters) and trigrams (triplets). The table in Fig. 2 shows these and has the most frequently occurring group at the head of each column. The second entry in each column gives the next most common group and so on.

Single letters	Digrams	Trigrams
E	TH	THE
T	IN	ING
A	ER	AND
O	RE	ION
N	AN	ENT
I	HE	FOR
S	AR	TIO
R	EN	ERE
H	TI	HER
L	TE	ATE
D	AT	VER
C	ON	TER
U	HA	THA

Figure 2   The Most Common Letter Groups in English

Aggression

A war game

Aggression is a war-game for two players. Each has 100 armies to be distributed in certain countries on a map which is drawn at the start of the game. A series of battles are then fought with the object of neutralising enemy armies. The player retaining control of the most countries is the winner. There are three phases, in each of which the same player moves first.

Phase 1: The players take turns to delineate one country on the map. This is done by drawing the boundary lines of a single enclosed area on a piece of plain paper. There are no restrictions on the size, shape or location of the countries, though it is recommended that they be drawn reasonably large. Twenty countries are to be drawn in the standard size game. Fig. 1 shows a typical map at the end of phase 1. The countries have been given letter-names to aid play in phase 3 but they are not essential to the game and may be omitted.

Phase 2: The players take turns to allocate some of their armies to one unoccupied country. The number of armies allocated is written into the country concerned and that country is then regarded as occupied. The player taking first turn should identify his own allocations by boldly under-lining his figures. Phase 2 continues until all countries are occupied or until both players have allocated all of their 100 armies. Fig. 2 shows the map at the end of phase 2 in a typical game to be played by Napoleon and Wellington. Note that Napoleon has favoured a small number of strong countries while Wellington has distributed his armies to a larger number of countries with relatively fewer armies in each. Countries B and N have been left unoccupied.

Phase 3: The players now take turns to conquer one or other of the opponent's countries. A country may be conquered if there are more of your armies in adjacent countries than your opponent has in the country under attack. Similarly your opponent may conquer one of your countries, at his turn, if he has a superiority of armies in adjacent countries. To qualify as "adjacent", countries must have a visible length of common boundary. Thus, in the figures, countries M, B, and D are adjacent to A, while countries A, M, K, F, C and D are all adjacent to B, and so on. The number of armies in the conquered country is crossed out and they take no further part. The armies carrying out the attack are in no way depleted and may be used for other attacks later in the game.

The object of the game is to retain more of your own occupied countries than the opponent retains of his. Note that countries you conquer don't contribute to your score but merely reduce your opponent's score by one as he will have retained one less country at the end of the game.

Fig. 3 shows the course of phase 3 of the Napoleon-*v*-Wellington campaign. The table is added to illustrate the sequence of moves. Napoleon took first turn and his armies are therefore underlined. The game finished with Napoleon holding four of his original countries and Wellington holding six of his original countries. Wellington's strategy of starting with more occupied countries than his opponent paid off although Napoleon did the most conquering. Wellington was the winner by two countries.

Strategy : A considerable amount of mathematical analysis of Aggression is possible but is not included here. The best strategy depends, in complex ways, upon the original map. It is possible to enjoy the game, and play well, without going into higher mathematics. Several tips are:

a Create "buffer" countries to protect weak countries during phase 2.

b Avoid crowding enemy-held countries at the start of phase 3.

c The first countries to attack in phase 3 are not necessarily the strongest of the enemy-held countries, but those which, by teamwork, can most damage your position.

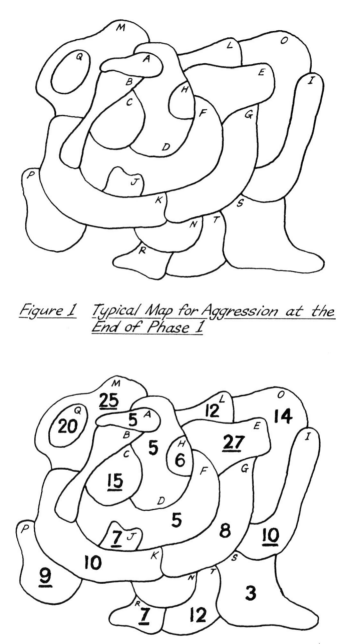

Figure 1   *Typical Map for Aggression at the End of Phase 1*

Figure 2   *Map for Aggression at the End of Phase 2*

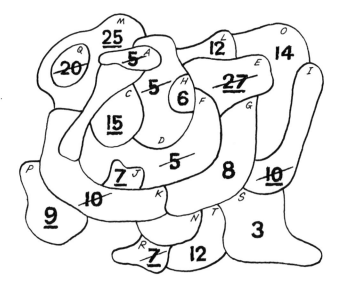

Napoleon (armies underlined) moved first

$$
\begin{array}{rcl}
M & \text{conquers} & Q \\
G, O, L & " & E \\
P, J & " & K \\
O & " & I \\
J & " & F \\
T & " & R \\
M & " & A \\
\end{array}
$$

At this stage Wellington is unable
to conquer any further countries.
The game finished with Napoleon's move:

C conquers D

Wellington won the game by retaining countries
H, L, O, G, T and S to Napoleon's M, P, J and C.

Figure 3   Map for Aggression at the End of
Phase 3

Battleships

A popular war game

There can be few of us who haven't played Battleships at some time or other. The original game is reputed to have been devised by British prisoners in Germany during the First World War and since then there have been variations on the rules, so it's necessary to specify the basic game before presenting the "de-luxe" version invented by Hubert Phillips. Mr. Phillips's main contribution was to introduce an element of investment into the first, or "setting-up", phase of the game. Both the basic and the more advanced game are for two players.

The basic game is started with each player indicating on a sheet of squared paper two 10-by-10 square frameworks by drawing a heavy border. He heads the columns of each framework with the letters A–J, and the rows by the numbers 1–10. Thus every square in a framework can be identified by a letter followed by a number. The top left-hand square is A1, the bottom right is J10. Fig. 1 shows a specimen sheet for the basic game. The top framework represents an area of sea containing the "home fleet". The lower framework is used to record the supposed positions of the "enemy fleet" and is filled in as the game proceeds.

Ships : The heavily drawn rectangles in the top framework of Fig. 1 represent ships which a player has drawn at the beginning of the game. Each player takes care to hide the exact disposition of his fleet from his opponent, in fact a player's sheet must not be seen by his opponent until the end of the game. A fleet comprises :

> 1 Battleship (4 squares)
> 2 Cruisers (3 squares each)
> 3 Destroyers (2 squares each)
> 4 Submarines (1 square each)

The squares denoting a ship must be drawn in a straight line. That is, there may be no L-shaped battleships or cruisers. No two ships may touch, not even at a corner.

Object: The object of Battleships is to sink the entire enemy fleet. This is done by firing "Salvoes" which consist of three shots. To sink a ship it is necessary to obtain a hit on *every one* of its constituent squares.

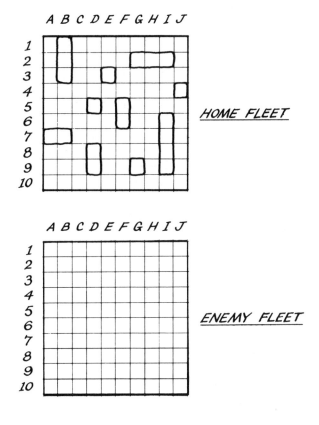

 Figure 1 *Game Sheet for Basic Battleships with Specimen Dispositions*

Salvoes: A salvo consists of three shots fired into named squares of the enemy's sea area. The players take turns to fire a salvo and after each the recipient of the shots must report any and all hits recorded. Note that the total number of hits is to be stated, *not the result of each individual shot* in the salvo.

As an example, suppose that you have set up your fleet as shown in Fig. 1. Your opponent fires a salvo by calling out "I7, E3 and C10." You must reply "One hit on a battleship, and one hit on a submarine." To record these hits on your own sheet you would strongly shade square I7 in the battleship, and square E3 which is the submarine. A ship is sunk only when every one of its squares has received a hit, so your submarine is sunk but the battleship still has three squares left. Your opponent does not know which of his three shots struck what at present and he must use some later salvoes to find and destroy your vessel. Considerable skill is involved in distributing shots in an economical way.

The manner of recording hits by your own salvoes on the lower framework of the sheet is a matter of personal preference. After each shot of a salvo you can place a clearly visible dot in the square you have named. If your opponent replies "no hits" you will know that all three squares are sea and you can write a cross into each square. If some hits are registered you can write lower case letters into the squares to denote the type of ship. Further salvoes directed near to these squares will enable you to eliminate some of the possibilities by progressively crossing out the letters. Definite hits can be shaded.

Note that in the basic game the number of salvoes is unlimited. The players shoot away until one or other fleet is entirely sunk.

The essential differences between the basic game and Hubert Phillips's[1] variation are as follows:

1 The playing area is larger, having 21 columns lettered A–U and 21 rows numbered 1–21.

[1] The author is grateful to Arco Publications for permission to describe this game, which was presented in *More Indoor Games for Two Players* by Hubert Phillips.

2 Each player starts the game with 160 "points". These are used to purchase ships and salvoes. Thus one player may choose to have many ships and few salvoes, and another the reverse. The setting-up is still done secretly so that no player knows how the other has spent his points. Since the number of salvoes is limited it's rare that a fleet is completely sunk. The winner is the player having the *highest points value of unsunk shipping* when both players have used up all their weapons of offence.

3 In addition to ships and salvoes further elements enter the game. These are reconnaissance planes, bombers, anti-aircraft guns, land in units of 3 by 3 squares, and an additional type of ship—the aircraft-carrier. The points-price and function of each of these is revealed in the next section below. All are positioned on the home-fleet framework at the start of the game in the same way as the ships.

Elements of the game : The purchase of these elements is entirely optional, though Hubert Phillips specifies that between 60 and 100 points must be spent on ships. You'll find that it's possible to play many interesting games without this restriction. Of course, if one player was to spend all his points on shipping the action would be somewhat one-sided. A player who spent all his points on offensive material could not win, and he would have to sink the entire enemy fleet to gain a draw.

1 *Ships* Cost : 1 point per square.
    Symbol : Surround the position with a heavy line as in the basic game.

The aircraft-carrier, which occupies an area of 2 by 2 squares and costs 4 points, may also be used. The other types of ship are as described in the basic game.

2 *Salvoes* Cost : 1 point each.
    Symbol : These are not written on to the sea framework. They are recorded at the side of the sheet and crossed off as they are used. See Fig. 3.

3 *Land* *Cost:* Land is free.

Symbol: Land must be placed in units of 3 by 3 squares which are lightly shaded. Land units may touch each other in any way. A diagram showing some land is included under the following elements.

4 *Recce planes* *Cost:* 1 point each.

Symbol: R.

Recce planes are placed on land squares or on squares within aircraft carriers. A player may use his turn to despatch one recce plane to a named square. His opponent must then tell him his exact dispositions within the 3 by 3 area surrounding the named square unless he is able to use an anti-aircraft gun to shoot down the recce plane. Note that any recce plane may be sent on a mission but it may be used only once. It must be crossed out *immediately* after use. Fig. 2 shows a portion of the home fleet area with several used recce planes and illustrates a plane being sent to square C4 of the enemy fleet area. The recce plane sees several items of interest and the conversation would go something like this:

Home player: "I'm sending a recce to C4."

Opponent: "Well—reading from left to right you see one square of a cruiser, and two squares of sea. On the next row you can see nothing but water! On the last row you see a land-square with a recce plane on it, another land-square, and finally a submarine. And don't forget to cross out that recce plane."

5 *Bombers* *Cost:* 3 points each.

Symbol: B

Bombers are placed on land squares or on squares within aircraft carriers. A player may use his turn to despatch one bomber to a named square in the enemy sea area. The bomber destroys all enemy units within the 3 by 3 area surrounding the named square. The opponent is required to report the total damage, not the exact squares where hits have been registered. Any bomber may be despatched but it may be used only once.

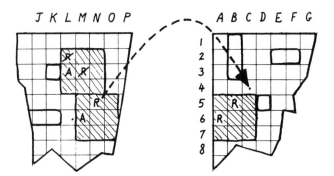

Figure 2   *Battleships –*
A Recce Plane is sent to C4

As an example, suppose that a bomber had been sent to square C4 in Fig. 2. The opponent would reply "One hit on a cruiser, one hit on a recce plane, and one submarine sunk."

6   *Atom Bombers*   *Cost :* 10 points each.
                 Symbol : X

An atom bomber is used exactly as an ordinary bomber but destroys all enemy units within the 5 by 5 area surrounding the square to which it is despatched. The opponent is required to report only the total damage and not the disposition of his units hit. Atom bombers are expensive but are immune from anti-aircraft fire from the AA guns described next.

7   *AA Guns*   *Cost :* 1 point each.
           Symbol : A

AA guns must be located on land. They are not permitted on aircraft carriers. They are used to shoot down recce planes and ordinary bombers. A "shot-down" recce plane cannot report any enemy positions, and similarly a "shot-down" bomber causes no damage. An AA gun can shoot down either of the above types of aircraft if it is sent to any square within the 3 by 3 area, of which the AA gun is the centre. Thus an AA gun sited at square B5 in Fig. 2 could have shot down the recce plane sent to C4, but an AA gun sited on A5 could not. Like the other units an AA gun can be used only once and must then be crossed out.

Fig. 3 shows a game-sheet for Hubert Phillips's game of Battleships after the player has marked the disposition of his forces but before any shooting has occurred. An inventory in the style of the following (which relates to Fig. 3) should be prepared before the sheet is set up. Needless to say, it should be carefully shielded from the prying eyes of the "enemy".

Inventory of Forces used in Figure 3

Ships	Aircraft carriers	2	Points	8
	Battleships	4	Points	16
	Cruisers	4	Points	12
	Destroyers	10	Points	20
	Submarines	16	Points	16
Other units	Recce planes	20	Points	20
	AA guns	16	Points	16
	Bombers	6	Points	18
	Atom bombers	2	Points	20
	Salvoes	14	Points	14
			Total points	160

Strategy : The logistics of this game cannot be discussed here in detail for reasons of space. Briefly, however, it should be carefully noted that each player's score at the end of the game is the total points value of his un-sunk shipping and not merely the total number of remaining ships as in the basic game. Thus, a battleship on which, say, three hits have been recorded is still worth four points at the end of the game. It is advisable always to buy some salvoes for "mopping up" operations after targets have been spotted. A very thorough analysis has been provided by Hubert Phillips.

Finally, remember that the success, and your enjoyment, of the game depends upon accurate recording and reporting by both players. Careful reporting is vital.

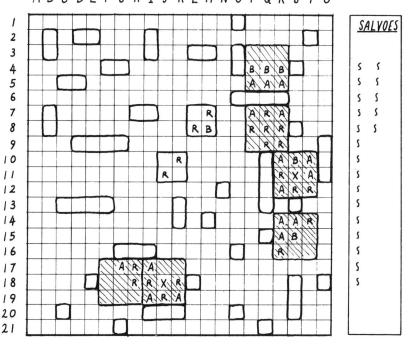

Figure 3   Sample Disposition of Material at
start of Battleships – Lower
Framework of Game Sheet not shown

Hangman

A word game for children

This simple game has been played by schoolchildren for many years. It's principally a game for junior and has considerable educational value, though don't let him know it! Any number can play and one person thinks of a word of about five or six letters. This person writes a number of dashes equal to the number of letters in his word. The other players take turns to guess one letter which might occur in the secret word. If a player is successful in guessing a letter which does form part of the word, that letter is written above the dash which corresponds with its position in the word. If the same letter occurs more than once in the word it is nevertheless written at only one of the allowable positions. Thus the

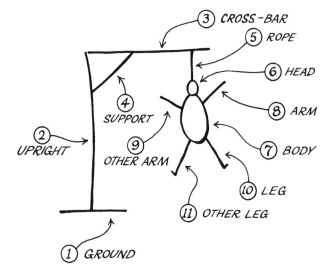

Figure 1   Hangman – The Picture to be Drawn

same letter may have to be guessed more than once. If a player fails to guess one of the letters in the word he is penalised by having to draw the next stage of a picture portraying a gallows with a hanging man. Any player who completes his picture before the word is fully discovered is "hanged" and takes no further part in that round.

Fig. 1 shows the construction of the picture of the hanging man. The parts of the picture are numbered and described to show the drawing-order.

Go-Moku

An ancient positional game

We generally find Go-Moku described in books on the Oriental game of Go. Go started in China as Wei Ch'I some 4,000 years ago and it's possible that Go-Moku is nearly as ancient. Both games are normally played on a Go board of 18 by 18 squares.

Go involves the capture of pieces and the subsequent reoccupation of their positions, so is not suitable as a pencil-and-paper game. Go-Moku does not involve capture and is easily played on squared paper. This game, which is for two players, has been played in the West since about 1880 under a variety of names such as Peggity, Pegfive and Spoil Five.

It's recommended that the "board" be a piece of squared paper having 19 squares in each direction and that the "pieces"—noughts and crosses—be written inside the squares. (On a proper Go board the pieces are played on to the intersections of the lines, not into the squares. Thus there are 19 positions in each direction.) The player marking "cross" moves first and the symbols are written one at a time and alternately into any of the empty squares. The object is to be the first player to obtain a straight line of exactly five contiguous symbols, of the same kind, on a row, column or diagonally. Each player is assumed to have an unlimited number of symbols at his disposal (181 in practice!).

Features of play: The rules are quite simple but play can nevertheless be highly sophisticated. Any player who obtains a line of four symbols with a blank square at either end is likely to win on his next move as his opponent cannot block both ends in one move. Such a line is called an "open-four". Many authors state that an open-four gives an automatic victory, but this isn't so. If a player has an open-four with another of his symbols in line but removed one square from

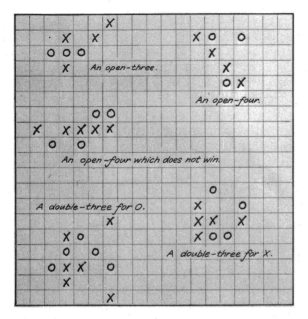

Figure 1 *Go Moku Sheet with some Typical Situations*

an end of the line, his opponent merely plays at the other end of the open-four to prevent his win. This is so because if the owner of the open-four then plays into the remaining square at the end of his line he obtains six symbols in a row, which does not qualify as a line of five symbols.

An "open-three" is a line of three symbols, of the same kind, with open space at either end. Unless the opponent blocks one end an open-three can become an open-four, so to avoid winning as the result of an oversight, which is no fun for anyone, it's customary to call "three" after forming an open-three.

Another commonly occurring situation is known as a "double-three". This is an intersecting pair of lines of three symbols each. In advanced play the formation of double-threes is prohibited if both threes could be developed into open-fours. But it's best to ignore this rule while learning the game. Fig. 1 fully illustrates some of the common situations.

Strategy : Once again we have a game with very simple rules in which surprisingly little is known regarding winning strategy. Most games are played near the centre of the sheet, and winning lines are often formed near the edge of the "busy" area where many symbols have been placed. So when playing to lay a foundation rather than executing a definite tactical plan, it's advisable to play in this boundary region, tending, as it were, to surround your opponent.

One golden rule applicable to this and all games of skill is "When in doubt, play to complicate the situation."

Subterfuge

A spy game with secret bidding

Subterfuge is a new spy game postulating a most unethical gang of secret agents who are entirely motivated by bribes recorded secretly by the players. These agents are lazy devils and remain at fixed positions on the game-sheet. All they do is to post some stolen plans to one another under the direction of the players. At any time an agent is working only for the player who has paid him the highest bribe.

Each player starts the game with an identical sheet of paper on which is drawn a chess-board pattern of squares. There are nine squares down and nine squares across and all but the corner and centre squares contain the identity numbers of secret agents. The agents are used to transfer some stolen plans—the "papers"—from Geneva, located at the centre of the squared pattern to one or other of the corner squares. Each player acts for one of the powers interested in acquiring the papers. The top left-hand square is London and "home" for the British player. The other corners are, in clockwise order, Moscow, Peking and Washington. There may be two, three or four players.

The players take turns and have the choice of doing one of two things as follows (it is not permitted to pass your turn):

1 Bribe one of the agents with an amount of £1 or more.
2 Move the papers from the agent currently holding them to an agent in an adjacent square.

The capital available to each player for making bribes is limited to £1,000.

Bribes: To execute a turn of type 1 you secretly write the amount of your bribe in the square corresponding to the agent concerned. You then deduct this amount from your capital in hand and indicate that it's the next player's turn.

It is important to note that existing bribes cannot be increased by the addition of money. If you feel that a bribe is too small you must make a brand-new bribe for the particular agent you wish to subvert. Your previous bribe money is totally lost.

Moves: A turn of type 2 is taken by simply stating that you are moving the papers from, say, agent 10 to agent 11. Agent 10 must be holding the papers at the start of the turn and 11 must be in a square adjacent to 10. An adjacent square is one which can be reached without crossing any other square. Squares in the middle of the sheet have eight adjacent squares and those at the corners have three. Thus the papers move like a king in chess. You win when you succeed in moving the papers from one of the agents adjacent to your home town into your home town. The easiest way to record the route taken by the papers is to draw a smooth connected line through the squares. The line is extended each time someone succeeds in moving the papers. Note the word "succeeds"; not all moves are successful, which brings us to the point of the game.

Challenges: Suppose one of your opponents moves the papers from 11 to 21. If you have a fair-sized bribe on 21 you'll probably not object to being made a present of the papers in this way. But suppose you have a bribe on 11, perhaps it is a large bribe. You will probably wish to object to your opponent giving instructions to "your" man 11 and this is just what you are entitled to do. Such an objection is called a challenge. You are challenging the validity of your opponent's move. Now there's a problem: how do you resolve who definitely owns 11? Who has, in fact, placed the largest bribe in the square marked 11? The obvious way to discover this is for both your opponent and yourself to announce the value of your bribes. The trouble with this method is that it reveals the size of the largest bribe, after which anybody will know what sum of money they must bid to gain control of 11.

Resolving ownership : After the challenge, one of the players, it does not matter whom, asks the other "Can you beat £10?" The actual amount stated must be less than the questioner's bribe on the agent concerned, say 11. If the other player has bribed 11 with a sum greater than £10 he replies "Yes". The questioner now repeats the question but quoting a larger sum of money, which must still be less than his bribe. The other player replies, and so it goes on, the sum quoted slowly rising, until one player or the other can go no further. Thus at the end of the discourse the players know only which of the two owns 11 and roughly the amount of the losing bribe. At this point there may be other players who want to continue the challenge starting at the sum last mentioned. Here is an example of a challenge: there are four players, John who has placed £45 on the agent 11, Mary who has placed £65, Harry who has placed £110 and Jill who has no bribe at all on 11. The challenge is first made by John when Mary tries to pass the papers from 11 to 21. This is how the challenge was resolved.

> Mary: "I move the papers from 11 to 21."
> John: "I challenge that—11 is working for me."
> Mary: "Can you beat £10?"
> John: "Easily, you'll have to do better than that."
> Mary: "OK, can you beat £25?"
> John: "Yes."
> Mary: "How about £40?"
> John: "Yes, I can beat that."
> Mary: "Can you beat £50?"
> John: "No, I'm sorry to say I can't."

At this point Harry, who has £110 on 11, decides to take up the challenge. He does not have to do so if he doesn't wish, of course.

> Harry: "Hold your horses Mary, I want to challenge your move. Can you beat £65?"
> Mary: "Well, I can't exactly beat it. Can you?"
> Harry: "Certainly, so you've been successfully challenged."

Note that Harry's large bribe of £110 is still a secret. Jill took no part in this challenge.

Result of a challenge : It isn't difficult to guess what happens next. Mary, who has lost the challenge, must return the papers to 11 and effectively loses her turn. If the challenge, made jointly by John and Harry, had been unsuccessful then Mary would have been awarded an extra turn. She might have used this to consolidate the papers with agent 21 by placing a large bribe on him, or she might have attempted to get the papers even nearer to home by moving them from 21 to some other agent. Note that the latter turn may itself have been challenged. Any turn of type 2 may be challenged. Obviously, nobody can challenge the placing of a bribe.

Challenging order : When a player has moved the papers, every other player has the right to challenge the move but the challenges must be issued *in the normal order of play.* That is, the player sitting on the mover's left is given the first option to challenge. If he chooses not to challenge the move, or if he fails in his challenge, the next player sitting on the latter's left is allowed to challenge, and so on. In the sample round of challenges above, the players were sitting in the order Mary, John, Harry and Jill. After the challenging is over the next player to move is the person sitting on the left of the last mover, not the last challenger. In the example the next person to move would have been John who was sitting on Mary's left.

Strategy : What's the best strategy for winning Subterfuge? If that were easy to answer there would be little interest in the game. Perhaps the over-riding factor is the psychology of one's opponents. Some players favour a bold, direct approach. They will quickly place large bribes on the agents leading straight from Geneva to their home town and will try to rush the papers there. It requires only one player to place one high blocking bribe on their path and the "hustler" will be in trouble. He will have spent most of his money and the papers will have been taken off the path occupied by his "safe" agents. If there are more than two players, however, there is the danger that each player will leave it to the others to arrange the blocking bribe. As a rule beginners make the error of spending too little and are usually easy prey for the hustler. As regards the start of the game it should be noted that since the papers are handed from agent to agent they cannot re-visit the Geneva square. Thus the player who first moves them towards his home town has something of an advantage over the player diagonally opposite him. The latter player will have to take a more roundabout route.

Variations: There's nothing sacrosanct about the rules presented here and you should feel free to try variations. For instance you could play the game on a much larger sheet, say 15 squares by 15 squares, and allocate a larger sum of money

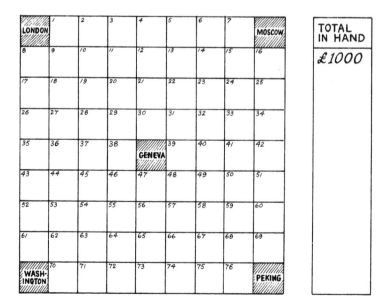

Figure 1   *Game Sheet for Subterfuge*

to each player. Another variation which leads to a longer game is to prohibit diagonal moves. The papers would be restricted to moving one square along a rank or a file.

Game-sheet : The best way to prepare a stock of game sheets is to re-draw the figure shown here at a larger scale and then produce copies on an electrostatic or photographic copying machine.

Letter-Strings

A simple word game

A fairly large sheet of paper, preferably lined, is needed for this simple word game which can be played by any number of people. The first player turns the paper so that its longest edge forms the top of the sheet and writes a single letter in the centre of the sheet. The players now take turns, in a clockwise order, to carry out one of the following actions:

1 Add *one* letter at either end of the string of letters stretching across the sheet.
2 Add one letter as above and underline any single English word formed of contiguous letters, backwards or forwards, which can be seen within the letter string, provided the word has not already been marked in this way. The player adds to his score a number equal to the number of letters in the word.
3 Underline any single word as above and score accordingly, *without* adding a letter to the string.

The winner is the player first reaching a score of 50, or any other agreed number of points.

Word formation: It is important to understand what constitutes a valid word in the context of this game. A word may be scored in moves of types 2 and 3 provided that it differs *in at least one letter* from any previously scored word. Here are some examples of permissible scoring words. Rather than underline, the words have been repeated underneath their positions in the string. The number in brackets represents the amount to be added to the score of the player marking the word.

ICABSOXILL

	a	(1)
	cab	(3)
	cabs	(4)
i		(1)
	so	(2)
	ox	(2)
	i	(1)
	ill	(3)

In this example it would have been quite in order for a player to mark the A in CAB *after* the word CAB had itself been marked.

As in the majority of word games, the marking of proper nouns, hyphenated words and words requiring an apostrophe, such as "DON'T", is not allowed. Single-letter words are permissible, though, which will tend to encourage the placing of the vowels I and A. Players may wish to permit the remaining vowels O, E and U to be marked as words scoring one point.

Strategy : The marking of long words of seven letters or more is a rare occurrence in this game so the regular accumulation of small scores is important. A good knowledge of the more unusual two- and three-letter words such as EM, TI, ZAX, etc., is an asset. Of course, a good dictionary should be on hand, though it shouldn't be scanned prior to a player's turn.

Letter-Strings may be played by two players at a fair level of sophistication, but with more players luck plays a larger part.

Buried Treasure

A game of bluff

Here is an easy game for children. It introduces the idea of bluff without requiring the players to lie! Buried Treasure is a game for two players but a third person is necessary at the start. Each player draws a square grid with rows and columns lettered and numbered as shown in Fig. 1. After one or two practice games the players will be able to dispense with the sheet and use only the letters and numbers.

The third (non-playing) person allocates four of the letters from A, B, C, D, E, F, G, H and I to one of the players and four of the remaining letters to the other player. Neither player knows what letters the other holds, or which of the letters is left over. The same procedure is used to allocate four of the nine numbers 1–9 to each player, one of the numbers being left over. The unallocated letter and number identify a square on the playing sheet in which treasure is buried and the players must try to find it. The first to announce the correct square is the winner.

The players take turns to do one of the following:

1 Ask the opponent if he holds a specified letter or number. The person asked *must* reply truthfully, but it's permissible for the player asking the question to enquire if the opponent holds a letter or number which is, in fact, held by the enquirer himself. The purpose is to mislead the opponent into thinking that the letter, or number, might be on the row or column of the buried treasure.

2 Suggest the position of the buried treasure. If the opponent holds one or both of the symbols suggested he merely replies "wrong" and takes his turn. It is not permitted to use bluff in this type of move. If the position specified is correct—that is, neither player holds either

of the symbols announced—the player quoting the position wins the game.

Fig. 1 shows a game sheet for Buried Treasure in which rows and columns may be marked as it's discovered that they could not lead to the treasure. The sheet is not really necessary for play and is primarily intended to show young players how the squares are identified by a letter and a number.

Strategy : Buried Treasure is hardly a game of skill, and yet it's often found that one player will win more frequently than the other! The players should watch for slight pauses and inflexions in speech, eye movements and so on when trying to

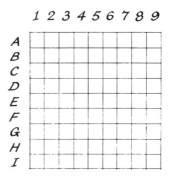

Figure 1   Game Sheet for Buried Treasure

decide if the opponent is bluffing. An appearance of confidence may succeed in rushing the opponent into a type 2 move which, if it fails in locating the treasure, gives him *less* information than a type 1 move.

The game is far more enjoyable if the treasure is something tangible like a toffee-apple.

The following pages contain playing grids for those games necessitating the more laborious preparation

Three-dimensional Noughts and Crosses

 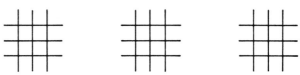

Think of a Letter

Crystals

Hex

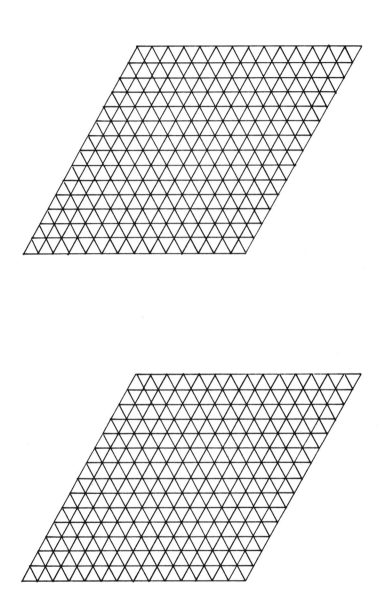

Battleships

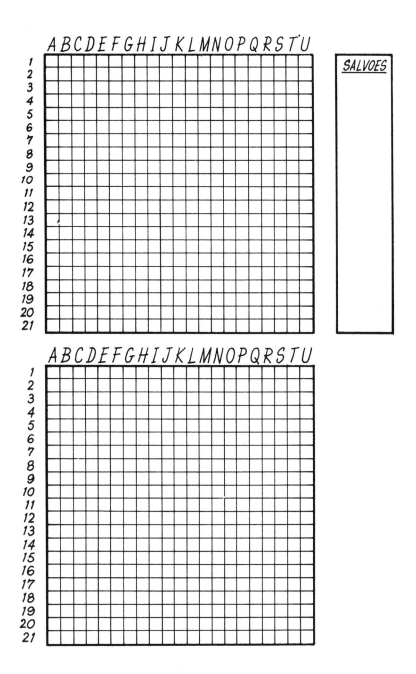

SALVOES

Go Moku

Subterfuge

LONDON	1	2	3	4	5	6	7	MOSCOW
8	9	10	11	12	13	14	15	16
17	18	19	20	21	22	23	24	25
26	27	28	29	30	31	32	33	34
35	36	37	38	GENEVA	39	40	41	42
43	44	45	46	47	48	49	50	51
52	53	54	55	56	57	58	59	60
61	62	63	64	65	66	67	68	69
WASH- INGTON 70	71	72	73	74	75	76		PEKING

TOTAL IN HAND
1000

LONDON	1	2	3	4	5	6	7	MOSCOW
8	9	10	11	12	13	14	15	16
17	18	19	20	21	22	23	24	25
26	27	28	29	30	31	32	33	34
35	36	37	38	GENEVA	39	40	41	42
43	44	45	46	47	48	49	50	51
52	53	54	55	56	57	58	59	60
61	62	63	64	65	66	67	68	69
WASH- INGTON 70	71	72	73	74	75	76		PEKING

TOTAL IN HAND
1000

Buried Treasure

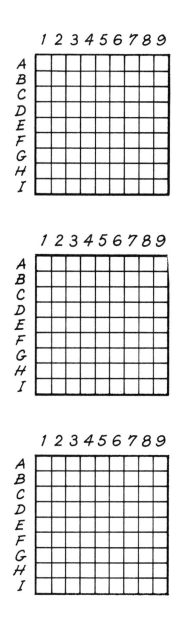